★ CONT]

CW01390399

PECULIAR PETS

2021

Words Of Wonder

Edited By Sarah Waterhouse

First published in Great Britain in 2021 by:

YoungWriters®
Est. 1991

Young Writers
Remus House
Coltsfoot Drive
Peterborough
PE2 9BF
Telephone: 01733 890066
Website: www.youngwriters.co.uk

Printed and bound in the UK by BookPrintingUK
Website: www.bookprintinguk.com
YB0478I

★ FOREWORD ★

Welcome Reader!

Are you ready to discover weird and wonderful creatures that you'd never even dreamed of?

For Young Writers' latest competition we asked primary school pupils to create a Peculiar Pet of their own invention, and then write a poem about it! They rose to the challenge magnificently and the result is this fantastic collection full of creepy critters and amazing animals!

Here at Young Writers our aim is to encourage creativity in children and to inspire a love of the written word, so it's great to get such an amazing response, with some absolutely fantastic poems. Not only have these young authors created imaginative and inventive animals, they've also crafted wonderful poems to showcase their creations and their writing ability. These poems are brimming with inspiration. The slimiest slitherers, the creepiest crawlers and furriest friends are all brought to life in these pages – you can decide for yourself which ones you'd like as a pet!

I'd like to congratulate all the young authors in this anthology, I hope this inspires them to continue with their creative writing.

Hartley Primary School, East Ham

Sivithi Balachandran (11)	50

Marsden Junior School, Marsden

Constance Stevenson (8)	51
Eve Clark (9)	52
Meredith Legge (8)	54
Scarlette Joanna-Rose Stevenson (10)	55
Catherine Farrell (10)	56
Bella Leinasars (10)	57
Iris Sykes (8)	58
Isobel Wagner (8)	59

Martock CE (VA) Primary School, Martock

Emily Anderton (8)	60
Wynter Cashen (8)	62
Mia-Rose Webber (8)	64
Elysa Dalwood (9)	65
Tia White (8)	66
Freya Studley (9)	67
Sienna Blackmore (9)	68
Aiden Baker (9)	69
Zeynep Akkurt (8)	70
Charlie Johnston (9)	71
Alfie Reynolds (9)	72
Molly Whitelock (9)	73
Maxwell Taylor (9)	74
Gracie-May Chapman (8)	75
Jacob Batten (8)	76
Olivia Cassell (9)	77
Alex Crabb (9)	78
Lexi Fane (8)	79
Elizabeth Clayton (8)	80
Isla Gould (9)	81
Jayden Ramsey (8)	82
Jack Galligan (8)	83
Lucas Paul Pike (9)	84
Mason Rendell (9)	85

Albie Fisher (8)	86
Layla Rendell (8)	87
Theo Taylor (8)	88
Diesel Hughes (8)	89
Ashton Mcguinness (8)	90
Connor Dervishi (8)	91
Mason Woodhouse (9)	92
Oliver Harding (8)	93
Ronnie Bouckley (8)	94
Freddie Frost (8)	95

Millbrook Combined School, High Wycombe

Ayesha Kanwar (7)	96
Amaya Qureshi (6)	97
Julia Gulacsi (6)	98
Gabriela Grudzinska (7)	99
Ruqaiyyah-Fatimah Kousar (7)	100
George Digby (7)	101

New Hall Primary & Children's Centre, Sutton Coldfield

Nyma Jawwad (10)	102
Ashia Hanley (10)	104
Elsie Taylor (9)	105
Joshika-Gauri Surgu (10)	106
Neva Giby (10)	107
Maksymillian (10)	108
Karma Salama (10)	109
Kawther Mahdi (10)	110

Nightingale Primary School, Hackney

Aaliyah Fasanya (8)	111
Gabriella Parker (8)	112
Khadijah Njie (8)	113
Maariyah Mirza (8)	114
Ryuto Hashimoto Huynh (8)	115

Perry Court E-ACT Academy, Hengrove

Tiffany-Lou Paget (10)	116

St Benedict's Catholic Primary School, Hindley

Tabitha Wright (9)	117
Isaac Wright (11)	118

St Gregory's Catholic Primary School, Margate

Natalia Campbell (7)	120
Annie Rajive (7)	121
Dami Olulode (7)	122
Poppy Queen (7)	123
Tatum Gower (6)	124
Swanika Kanesarasa (6)	125
Astrid Binu (7)	126
Emma Abraham (6)	127
Alana Hobley (7)	128

Wildground Junior School, Dibden Purlieu

Demi-Rose Marlow (8)	129
Eddie Anderson (8)	130
Isla Burrow (8)	131
Charlotte Newcombe (8)	132
Alba Bunday (8)	133
Elise Valman	134
Lucas Zaharia (7)	135
Hazel Baxter (8)	136
Ryan C Windebank (8)	137
Ethan Parker	138
Eleyna Carvalho (8)	139
Osea Kamakorewa (7)	140
Joe Hoyle	141
Theodore Knowlton (8)	142
Leo Mark Hamilton (8)	143
Roan Wells (8)	144
Molly Paddock (8)	145
Isaac Campbell (8)	146

Maiya Ferguson (8)	147
Hetty Bliss (8)	148
Bella-Rose Knightbridge (8)	149
Harley Baylis (7)	150
Evelyn Havers (8)	151
Jethro Kendie (8)	152
Heidi Woodhead	153
Noah Tollervey (8)	154
Leo Elsley	155
James McIldoon (7)	156
Emily Gahr (7)	157
Joseph Mitchell (7)	158
Tiana-Rae Smith (8)	159
Andrew-John Smith (8)	160

Woodlands School, Great Warley

Luke Ryan Spendlove (11)	161

THE POEMS

Crognon

He is rarer than a chameleon,
He is cooler than a lion,
Even though people call him odd,
He is still a part of my peculiar squad.
His face is a hawk,
It's stronger than a metal fork,
He has a long beak,
His friends call him the Champion Cheat,
He has cat ears,
He is so tremendously creepy,
Dogs are wary,
His ears are so sharp
That even his owner can't eat a Pop-Tart,
He has a baboon torso
He's so fat he has to go to Camp Fatso,
His owner's name was Ronald,
He just had McDonald's,
Crognon has frog legs,
He sleeps on two beds,
People call him creepy,
But actually, he's just very sleepy!

Adam Domineck (10)
Al Mizan School, London

Friendly Cat

A lady was biking down the road
When she saw a box
She looked inside and saw a fox
Wait, it's a cat! With it back home she rode
The cat was in a deep sleep
And very furry ginger
She realised it was hers to keep
She found the cat was a bit injured
She put a bandage on her and it made her better
Thirty minutes later, the cat started to wake up
All ready, the cat ran around and she let her
After that, she drank milk from a cup
That's how they became friends
And this is how the story ends.

Ayan Mintu (9)
Al Mizan School, London

Chiateow

Old Chiateow is partly a cat.
He also sits on a nice mat.

He doesn't want aid.
He just wants to be paid.
He's old Chiateow who is partly a cat!

Salmaan Al-Ameen (8)

Al Mizan School, London

Thrasher The Destroyer

T erminator

H umongous

R apid

A ssassin

S ly

H orrendous

E vil

R obotic.

Humza Ibn Kayum (10)

Al Mizan School, London

My Dog Gizmo

My dog, Gizmo, is blind; he cannot see.
But don't feel sorry, he can still be whatever he
wants to be.
He uses his nose to find his food.
If he bumps into you, he's not being rude;
It's because he cannot see like you.
He finds his water using his mat -
He can still find his drink
And he is happy about that.
Gizmo has been my dog all my life;
He's ten now. Don't feel sorry because he
Cannot
See.
Don't worry about him,
He has family
And is as happy
As can be.

Lexi Vining (10)
Berrow CE Primary School, Berrow

Star

Star is a doggy,
Chewing on his yummy treat,
Barking at the door.
Rub his tummy, he won't bite,
Playful, excitable dog.

Ellie Skelding (11)
Berrow CE Primary School, Berrow

Kitty Corn

A cat in a hat with a bat.

My Kitty Corn has a horn and loves corn.

My friend has a unicorn but it will never beat my Kitty Corn.

She wanders around and makes my neighbours go, "Don't be loud!"

But I don't care, because at night she takes flight

Over the clouds and not a sound can be heard from our mouths.

When we land and step on a soda can,

I walk to bed and sleep tight while my Kitty Corn takes flight.

Emma Kipps-Calderon (9)

Charles Dickens Primary School, Southwark

My Breathtaking Bunny

My bunny's name is Mr Twinkle Toes
And his ears are like a never-ending crazy hose.
They wave, they waft,
They're oh so soft.

Though, at night, he doesn't act the same,
He does not act so tame

And at the dead of night,
My body, it froze with fright,
As my marvellous pet had escaped!

I ran across the street
Like a shark seeking meat.
I peeked around a corner,
Where I saw a dinosaur foreigner.

My voice shook with horror. "Who are you?"
"I'm your pet!" the dinosaur said, picking up my
fallen shoe.
"Now don't you act funny, my pet is a bunny," I
laughed while staring blankly.

The dinosaur responded, "My name is Mr Twinkle
Toes, actually."
Was my pet a dinosaur?
An extinct animal who cried roar?
No matter, I decided,
I shall love him anyway.
And now we are inseparable;
I never want him to go away.

Asiya Elkhouli (10)
Charles Dickens Primary School, Southwark

The Story Of A Horse

I've forever wanted a horse,
Mum always says, "No way!"
I ask, "Why not? It's reasonable."
She says, "He'll whinny and bray."

I turn to her, my face bright red,
"But that's what horses do!"
I plead and plead and plead again,
I want a horse, I really do!

It isn't nearly Christmas,
My birthday isn't near,
But I still really want a horse,
My eyes soon shed a tear.

On Friday evening, 8 o'clock,
A van appears in red,
Mum goes outside, then comes back
And tells me, "Go to bed."

Next morning in my bedroom,
As I'm making up my bed,
I go downstairs and see my horse,
Behold, the horse is red!

Lana Havelock (10)

Charles Dickens Primary School, Southwark

Polly Uniphix

P olly Uniphix is my peculiar pet,

O ther pets are not like mine,

L oves me as much as I love her,

L ollipops are the only food she eats and she also watches TV.

Y ou now know about my crazy uni.

(PS, she's 100% allergic to fire!)

Rose Maung (10)
Charles Dickens Primary School, Southwark

Bobby!

B obby, big excavating thing.

O pal-blue eyes patterned with golden stars.

B arters with dangerous beings.

B eware of Bobby.

Y es, he is a big excavating thing with opal-blue, gold-patterned eyes.

Eliot Alevizou-Taylor (10)

Charles Dickens Primary School, Southwark

Sophia The Hat-Taker

There's a bundle in the jungle.
There's a whisper in the attic.
"She's waking up!" Scarlett cries.
"Where's my hat?" asks Lucy.
She's a clever clogs and colourful dog.
Always messy, gentle and lovely.
Cute and majestic and magical
Now I know where my stunning hat is!

Scarlett Bui (7)
Communicate Tutoring, Carlisle

Deathshaper

"Aww, Mummy, he's adorable, please can we get
him?"
Looking at the puppy, Mum looked very dim,
"Only if you always clean him up."
I nodded knowing how much I would love my new
pup.

Soon, my pup started to behave peculiarly
And, to my dismay, he grew ill,
When I thought he was going to go,
He formed my nightmare.

A deadly corpse rose from the cage in the store,
Peter the puppy was no more!
It caught me and sucked my insides out,
I was just a shell of a human and there was
nothing left to talk about.

Zahra Ishfaq (9)
Cranbrook Primary School, Ilford

Caramel The Dog

My birthday was a big surprise,
Receiving a toy dog called Poppy.
It was incredibly cute and floppy,
But no match for getting a real puppy.

On the way to the park,
We stopped at Harry's, the local pet store.
A pair of adorable eyes came bounding over to me,
Making my heart melt and beam.
I gave it a gentle hug and whispered, "Wish you
could be mine."

As I got back on my bike,
It followed me and took a hike.
In our excitement, its slimy tongue licked my face
in delight
Caramel was the perfect name to match its cream
and brown coat.

On the landing,
A pair of roller skates lay still.

Caramel sniffed and played with the shoes.
Suddenly, the skates flipped
And it took the skates across the room.

Jaseena Zaheen (8)

Cranbrook Primary School, Ilford

Jack And The Black Cats!

A day like any other
I woke up thirsty
I saw, we all saw
Jack, a messy, furry pile of fluff
He disappeared in a puff!

I saw Jack
With a magnifying glass
With a black cat in cuffs
Heading to the station
I huffed and puffed!
What could he possibly be doing?

I ran downstairs
Huffing and puffing
I didn't know what to do
First of all, I needed a clue!

I shouted, "Jack!"
I ran after him
He ran away

Entered the station
Me too!
Put the cat in a cell
And flew out of a window
Then flew home.

Seeyam Khan (8)

Cranbrook Primary School, Ilford

The Mysterious Dragon

This mysterious dragon rules all animals
It's so special because it's 10,000 years old.
Its breath's like the sun beating on everybody.
He has bat wings as long as ten
Limousines.
It's so cool that all the animals bow to
The mighty dragon.
Glistening rain falls on his face as
He's awakened from his slumber.
It's so mysterious, you can
Find it in its kingdom, deep in the
Inside world.

It's so dangerous, the mysterious
Dragon can eat you up in a gobble.

Hamza Ahmed (9)
Cranbrook Primary School, Ilford

Turbo Snail

He goes as fast as max speed.
He enters a race, he will always be in the lead.
His name is Tom!
The fastest in the world is him,
But even the fastest cheetah can't beat this
legendary machine.
He is the master of speed.
Don't dare ever, in your whole life, attempt to beat
him.
I would love to be him
But...
He is a snail, a gross slimy creature,
So he does have some disadvantages.
Sometimes he gets bullied, I mean who wouldn't
Really?
A fast snail.

Raees Pandore (9)
Cranbrook Primary School, Ilford

My Amazing Pet

A while ago, I adopted a dog,
When he was still little, he hopped like a frog,
He was brown like a log.

His eyes were sparkly blue,
He could look through and through,
At times, he did not know what to do,
But I always knew.

He was clever, supersonic,
He would put on his goggles and would fly
Like a comet.

The next night,
I crept out into the light,
There Tommy and I
Played and enjoyed in the darkness of the night.

Ibrahim Rai (9)
Cranbrook Primary School, Ilford

My Rainbow-Scaled Whale

R ainbow scales
A dorable skin
I ntelligent creature
N ever ferocious
B eautiful body
O ne of a kind
W ise whale

S wishing tail
C onfident in the sea
A ttractive attributes
L oyal companion
E nergetic splashing
D elightful diving

W arm whale
H armless horn
A wesome
L oving
E xciting.

Husna Shahid (9)
Cranbrook Primary School, Ilford

The Grange Giraffe

Giraffes are tall and lanky,
My giraffe can ride a cycle,
It can even do a turn,
It wears a huge helmet,
Sometimes its head bangs on a tree,
Whenever we go somewhere, it always gets a cycle.

We were down in the woods,
He came rushing with his speedy cycle,
All of a sudden, the cycle broke,
My giraffe kept trying to get it up
But no, it was all junk,
I taught him how to walk,
He was getting it but he kept falling down.

Abtahi Siddique (9)
Cranbrook Primary School, Ilford

My Super Shadow

My cat has a white moustache
She looks very smart...
But she is very silly!
Her favourite thing to do is to sleep!
She sleeps all day
Like a caterpillar in a cocoon
When we go to sleep is the time she wakes up.
She runs around the building
Looking for crime
She fights all the dogs
Like the ninja cat she is!
When the sun goes up, she goes back down
To her warm, snuggly bed
Tucked up with her blanket, purring away.

Sophia (8)
Cranbrook Primary School, Ilford

My Pet Octo

M y pet, Octo, is the best pet out there
Y es, he's the best

P eculiar he may be, though he's the best
E veryone thinks he's fake
T hat's because he only appears when I'm alone

O cto is an octopus, very smart and clever
C ute and extraordinary
T alented enough to breakdance!
O cto comes when I'm alone, but I'm never alone, not with him.

Shehran Khan (9)

Cranbrook Primary School, Ilford

My Dritten

Yesterday, I got a dritten,
She was so cute, I named her Mitten.
When it spread its wings, it wanted to play
So we played by flying night and day.

All she ate was kitten food,
Humour was always in her mood.
She only hugged people she liked,
She always did it on our hikes.

Soon, Mitten got so ill
She started lying down so still.
She was impossible to fix and mend.
Rest in peace, my little friend.

Zara Ayubson (8)
Cranbrook Primary School, Ilford

The Long-Tailed Dog!

As sly as a fox, as fast as a robot.
She was a cute, fluffy, silly puppy.
Oh, she was clever, spiky, brave
And messy!

Some of her favourite things are:
Playing in mud, flowing of her tail
And being on TV.
But she hates to get a wash
And to get dry.

Her tail is as long as a hall with
Four mountains on top and six
Enormous trees on top!
Most people say, "What a long tail!"

Carmina Podaru (9)
Cranbrook Primary School, Ilford

Dunny The Peculiar Bunny

Dunny is a very peculiar type of pet,
In fact, he is one of the odd pets out in his pet's
vet.

Dunny is a bunny,
But...
When you get to know him, he's got an attitude.
When I say attitude, I mean *attitude*.

Dunny had so many odd friends like him
But did you expect him to be rude to them?

Pfft... No
Don't judge anyone by their attitude,
They change.

Hibah Sultan (9)
Cranbrook Primary School, Ilford

Problem-Solving Pangolin

P angolins are an engineer's best friend,
A lways fixing or finding solutions,
N ever giving up, persevering till the end,
G reat at designing super inventions,
O rder a problem solver and a pangolin will be there,
L oved by everyone absolutely everywhere,
I nventive, intelligent and amazing,
N ever letting anyone down, ensuring machines are behaving.

Sulaiyman Zaid Siddiqui (8)

Cranbrook Primary School, Ilford

Beecat Freedom!

F or every day, my cat comes to me

R eally, she is a special cat, her name is Beecat.

E xactly how I wanted her,

E specially when we're in the garden and she gets freedom.

D one with the day, I go to sleep, she sleeps on top of me.

O h and one day she was at the window

M oving towards the curtain, I let her go and she flies away in the dark sky.

Inaayah Noori (9)

Cranbrook Primary School, Ilford

Perfect Pets

Pets are perfect and so is my pet.
My pet is a perfect pet
He is a fish.
He is the epitome of beauty
He's marvellous, clever, incredible, colourful, cool
and clever.
He's funny but fishy.
He can travel at 600mph
But gets tired.
He eats fantastic foods.
He is strong like a £100,000 car
That's bulletproof.
Who is he to me?
He's my friend.

Raihaan Shoaib (8)
Cranbrook Primary School, Ilford

Human Puppy

Poppy wants to be like humans,
But Poppy is a poodle
And when she tries to walk like them,
She always flops down like a noodle.

The hardest is clothes,
Mostly my pink dress,
It is so hard to put on,
Who knew it could be such a mess?

But the one thing Poppy is good at
Is how humans talk,
She is happy to have learnt that
Though she can't walk.

Aishah Ahmed (9)
Cranbrook Primary School, Ilford

The Perfect Dog For Me!

A while ago, I adopted a dog
Soon, he started to spin like a cog.
His name was Snowball
He was playful and joyful.

Even though he seemed normal
And he acted very formal,
His floppy ears made him look weird
But his mischievous eyes shone bright.

I took Snowball out for a walk in the night.
All of a sudden,
Snowball barked
And gave me a fright!

Wali Rai (9)
Cranbrook Primary School, Ilford

Our Pet

On Monday, we went to this pet shop called
Peculiar Pets
We went around and saw an llumfoxunidrag
We asked a pet keeper if they would allow us to
have the llumfoxunidrag
He said yes,
We took him home.
Tuesday, he started roaring
And flew away.
Wednesday, he came back
Thursday, when he started roaring, I held his tail
And we flew away.

Ryan Toofail (8)
Cranbrook Primary School, Ilford

The Silly Kitten

The furry kitten
Has been bitten
By an old ugly rat
That was hiding under a hat
That belonged to Mr Pounce,
So many hats you can't even count.

The cat was in a flat
It was on the mat
The cat was zen but not for long
The cat was in Hong Kong
But something went wrong
When the humming started, a song...

Eusebiu-Alin Alih Cristea (9)
Cranbrook Primary School, Ilford

Here She Comes! Caticorn!

C ameras get ready!

A mazing Caticorn is coming!

T oday is the day! A girl will give her a teddy!

I magine seeing Caticorn. I'm so excited.

C ome on! She is this way!

O h, wait till you see!

R emember, she is shy.

N ever scare her. Why? Remember, she is shy...

Chloe Portbury (9)

Cranbrook Primary School, Ilford

My Flying Sheep

My pet was a flying sheep called Jay
Who liked to eat yellow-coloured hay.
He flew to the top of a mountain
To have a drink from a beautiful fountain.
There he met a gigantic brown bear,
They formed a friendship in the lair
With tea and biscuits, enough to share
And I never saw Jay the sheep again.

Jay Mistry (9)
Cranbrook Primary School, Ilford

The Coolest Cat In Town

K ind, loving, adorable kitten

I love my kitten just like she loves me

T errific fashionista, she looks so fabulous

T ime for my kitten to strut her fashionable ways

E xcited cats all around, waiting to see something new

N ever a bad fashion moment for this cool cat.

Safoorah Siddiqui (8)

Cranbrook Primary School, Ilford

My Pet Dog

I have a dog,
He looks like a log,
My dog lets out a woof
And is gone with a poof,
Where'd he go?
I see him
Dancing around on his four furry legs,
Not making a sound,
He looks at me,
Sees me,
He runs away
And leaves a waffle
And that's why he's called Waffle.

Vansh Shandilya (9)
Cranbrook Primary School, Ilford

A Peculiar Pet

Last week, I adopted a wolf.
She is cute and cuddly and grey
Like my coat.
But when the sun goes down
She sits up straight and
Howls at the glistening moon
Every night.
Then we start to talk about
Our feelings.
A peculiar pet she is.
But to me, she is perfect.

Khadijah Aya Ali (8)
Cranbrook Primary School, Ilford

Monster Corn

M alicious soul
O bnoxiously cute
N ever nice
S our-hearted
T iny, tamed
E erie-eyed
R adical, rampaging

C ocky mind, outgoing
O ddball body
R otten to the core but
N ever lets you down.

Zakiyyah Sarpanch (9)

Cranbrook Primary School, Ilford

The Silly Cat

A silly cat
Went in the garden,
He jumped in the bin,
He shouted, "Miaow, miaow!"
Someone appeared, they helped it out,
The cat went in the house,
He found a hole, he put his head in,
Now he regrets his decision once again.

Aron Gradica (9)
Cranbrook Primary School, Ilford

Acrostic Poem About Speedy

S uper fast

P olite gentleman cat

E nthusiastic and lazy

E ntertaining in the garden

D oing something messy and getting dirty with mud.

Y ou're so fast.

Bogdan Tugulea (9)

Cranbrook Primary School, Ilford

Peculiar Tommy

T roublemaker

O ld

M otivated

M astermind

Y ou will love him.

Adam Abdul-Ghaffar (8)

Cranbrook Primary School, Ilford

The Flying-But-Scared Caterpillar

My peculiar pet is always at the vet.
He is smooth and he is sometimes in the groove.
Whenever he starts to fly, he starts to cry.
When he is in the air, he starts moving like he's on stairs.
When he goes high, after a few seconds, he starts to go below the sky.
So that is why my pet doesn't like to fly.

Ayaz Sadikali (8)
Days Lane Primary School, Sidcup

My Musical Mouse

He is small and as white as paper,
He wears a minuscule tuxedo and has no haters,
He is rotund with a tiny pink nose,
While formally dressed, for photos he will pose,
But this furry little cheek has a secret,
I only just found this out, quite recent.
He is a *musical mouse!*
At night, he sings at the Opera House!
At night, he tapdances!
What are the chances?
Harrison, the mouse.
The name that shall go down in history!

Lily-Mai Smith (11)

Downham CE (VC) Primary School, Ramsden Heath

Clever Mrs Ivy

Mrs Ivy, my pet sheep,
Is very clever,
Sometimes I think she never goes to sleep,
I'll love her forever and ever.

She always knows when I open the gate,
She's very funny,
She hates having to wait,
Especially if it's sunny.

Cheese rolls are her favourite,
She likes chocolate biscuits too,
She'll eat up every little bit,
And cheers me up whenever I'm blue.

Jessica Wakefield (8)
Grendon CE Primary School, Grendon

Bella The Buttercat

Bonny Bella is a clever cat
Who sat reading on a mat.
She wanted to fly
Like a butterfly in the sky.
She kicked her tiny feet
Which are oh so sweet
She pushed off into the air
With her wings that are a pair
She flew up with the birds
And she had no words.

Violet French (8)
Grendon CE Primary School, Grendon

My Pawsome Puppy

It lurked in the dark
Then it started to bark
We thought it could be violent
But then it went silent

Day after day, we had to hear the horrible sounds
Hurting our precious ears
Could it possibly/surprisingly be a hound?
However, it was never found!

We finally decided to let it come in
And it was very muddy
But all this time, it had been
An adorable little puppy!

Sivithi Balachandran (11)
Hartley Primary School, East Ham

Venger And The Dragon

Venger is a peculiar pet who truly does inspire,
He's part sheep, butterfly, horse and pig and has teeth of a vampire.
Although he's made of all these parts,
His deadly weapon is his toxic farts!
One day, an angry dragon came swooping into town.
Like a bulldozer, he crashed about and knocked the houses down.
Venger didn't like this, it made him so upset.
He challenged the dragon to a duel, our brave heroic pet.
The battle didn't last that long, they fought like cat and dog,
Then Venger did an enormous trump that created a poisonous fog.
The dragon couldn't stand the whiff and tried to hold his breath,
But Venger's smelly toxic guff brought the dragon to his death!

Constance Stevenson (8)

Marsden Junior School, Marsden

The Talk

He lies
He wails
Convinces everyone on his little tales
He's small
He's kind
He's something you would never want to leave
behind
He's a Saint Bernard
A long, curvy tail
Cute, adoring eyes
Tells the best of stories
But most of them are lies
He can talk to anyone
Thanks to his magical mouth
But most people when they see him
Run away and brandish a terrible scream
One time he said, "Hello"
To a kind, little fellow
'Twas a girl
With a lovely curl
In her bright orange hair

She had a shocked voice
But said back, "Hello"
He was in a terrible delight
They played board games by lamplight
They became wonderful friends.

Eve Clark (9)
Marsden Junior School, Marsden

Painting Pig

P erfect pink pig as pretty as can be

A mazing and amusing, as perfect as can be

I maginative and interfering, as pink as can be

N othing is better than pretty pink.

T errific learning Painting Pig is better than you think.

I ncluding the paintings so wonderful and bright

N othing could be better than these pretty paintings.

G et a pig as gentle as can be, nothing can be better than Painting Pig

P eculiar, perfect pig, amazing for a pet

I sn't it beautiful, the painting and the pig?

G irls can choose if they want the pig or not and boys fight over having it with their massive shouting voices.

Meredith Legge (8)
Marsden Junior School, Marsden

Roxie The Rock Star Cat!

One day Roxie was passing by
And thought to give being a rockstar a try
Sadly the elephants heard what she said
And they replied, "You're too small, you can't even get out of bed!"
So she went to the competition with pride
She was that scared she almost died
She got on stage and heard the crowd
She couldn't wait to bow
She started to sing
And the guitar went off with a bing
And the crowd went wild
She remembered this moment from when she was a child
So she still sings to this day
You couldn't change her mind either way.

Scarlette Joanna-Rose Stevenson (10)

Marsden Junior School, Marsden

The Mismatched Cat

I have an amazing cat called Calamity
Which is not like any other
He's cooler than any other animal
There's more we're about to discover
He likes to play in the water
He likes to have a bath
He likes the sound of fireworks
We will sit and have a laugh
Walks are my cat's all-time favourite thing
It's something he'll never ban
But when no one is watching...
He flies like Superman!
So yes my cat's unusual,
He's fluffy like a sheep
But the only thing he fits in with
Is he loves and loves to sleep!

Catherine Farrell (10)
Marsden Junior School, Marsden

House Cish

Some people say I look a bit odd
I have pointy ears like a cat
And shiny scales like a cod!
I spend my days inside, that's where I like to be
Then when my humans are asleep, I go swim in the sea
I eat tuna from a tin when I'm in my house
Then on my way to the sea I snack on a mouse
I love my life, I do as I please
Playing with my toys, then gliding through the seas
Oh and one last thing before I forget
Do you know another cat that likes to get wet?

Bella Leinasars (10)
Marsden Junior School, Marsden

Rocker The Ravenous

R avenous Rocker raiding,

O n the counter lay the cupboard of food, don't go in or you'll leave your owner in a mood.

C *ats can do what they want*, thought Rocker, disobeying.

K eeps cantering out the door to the concert he adores, but footprints are on the clean floor!

E verything was great, Rocker was a star shining as bright as the sun.

R ocker became a pet celebrity and everybody loved him.

Iris Sykes (8)

Marsden Junior School, Marsden

Annoying Old Goat

G rumpy goat

R ude manners

U nbearable eater

F ence-breaker

F urious horns

A gile jumper

L arge loopy tail

I ncredible escape artist

F unny flower-eater

F rustrating his owners.

Isobel Wagner (8)
Marsden Junior School, Marsden

Me And Cutypie Off To The Caribbean Islands

Me and Cutypie, my hummingbird, were flying to the Caribbean Islands.
Cutypie eats fresh fruit, sap and nectar so sweet.
She is colourful, calm and cute.
She cleans my room, can make me small and can make herself big and can even make money out of thin air!
She can fly really, really fast and can make a pod that we can sleep in.

So we arrived in the Caribbean Islands and she made a pod really fast.
We slept.
In the morning, she turned into me and made some money and then went shopping.
She came back with a bleeding arm.
She flew up and talked to me about it.
It turns out she couldn't control her arm and cut it on the aisle.

I brought her to the vets, where they quickly fixed her up.
We then went to explore the rest of the island.

In a couple of days, we were flying back to England
Saying that was a good adventure we had together!

Emily Anderton (8)
Martock CE (VA) Primary School, Martock

My Fennec Fox, Cotton Ball

I was sat on my colourful bed, I went out to the
forest instead.
I went with my keyring,
My Cotton Ball is so very fluffy.
Then I put her on the floor and - wow!
She turned into her big furry self
Sometimes, when she's a keyring she says,
"When I'm a keyring, how are you feeling?"
And when people see me and my fox,
We're a big surprise.
Me and my fox on our daily exercise.
That's definitely my Cotton Ball.
But don't forget, she can be very wild and lazy,
We head west near the road.
"Oh!" I almost forgot, she can turn invisible,
Where's she gone?
Oh, there she is on the roof,
She jumps down like a parachute.
She munches and crunches while she blushes.

"See you next Tuesday," she said
And off she went.

Wynter Cashen (8)
Martock CE (VA) Primary School, Martock

Cheetah Corn

C heetah Corn is the best pet in the world.

H er favourite food is pizza with pepperoni that the people gave her.

E xcited a lot sometimes,

E specially when she goes to the cinema to watch movies.

T hen sometimes you can see her galloping on the pavement

A nd her favourite dessert is chocolate cake and custard.

H er cage is neon and pastel rainbow and when it's night, she glows.

C reatively, she made her bed with leaves and a new bed sheet that she found.

O nly at night she plays.

R eal glitter.

N ow if you see her, don't be shy, be friends with her, that's how it goes.

Mia-Rose Webber (8)

Martock CE (VA) Primary School, Martock

Pupstar And Me

I took my Pupstar to the studio.
On the way, he snacked on a potato.
Halfway there, he also ate a pear.
He takes me shopping,
I like it when he helps me do the washing.
He likes to cuddle,
He always plays in puddles.
He is so talented,
He makes me feel delighted.
He makes music,
He has never been sick.
Me and my Pupstar,
He's as good as a guitar.
We sing together,
He could do a bit better!
When we get back home,
I feed him a bone.
We both play the drums.
Then I eat a plum
And I say
To myself, *what a day.*

Elysa Dalwood (9)
Martock CE (VA) Primary School, Martock

My Pet Lamases Rocks!

I took my Lamases up to a fluffy cloud,
When we got there, she felt super proud
Because she'd never managed to get up here,
So I started to shed a huge tear.
But as I heard my mum wailing for me,
I kept as quiet as I could possibly be.
Soon after, I heard her go to sleep,
I still didn't make a single peep.
I leapt on Lamases' back and we flew very quickly down,
I felt a bit like the Queen but with no glorious crown.
Then Lamases transformed into a teddy bear
And one thing I will mainly do for Lamases
Is care very much about her.

Tia White (8)
Martock CE (VA) Primary School, Martock

Shop, Shop, Shop

Molly and me, we like to shop,
When it comes between us, we can't stop.
We buy some crisps, vegetables and fruits,
Then we buy cars that do loop-the-loops.

Now it's time for toothbrushes, toothpaste,
We'll buy it all, it will brighten up the place.
Quavers it is until we stop,
Orange and crispy, we'll take the lot.

Before we make a move, let's buy some bread,
Seedy or white, so many types to fill your head.
Molly and me go home to put our shopping away
Until it comes to another shopping day.

Freya Studley (9)
Martock CE (VA) Primary School, Martock

My Jello Jellyfish

I took my jello to my room,
He swept it up with a bushy broom.
My jello can clean up,
But his favourite is polishing the big cup.

I took him to the beach to see the sea,
He ate someone's pea.
He will die if he doesn't sting,
But when he stings, everyone goes into a floppy
fling.

The next morning, I woke up to a splash,
It sounded like someone very posh.
I went to see what was making the splish
When I realised my jello was now a normal jellyfish!

Sienna Blackmore (9)
Martock CE (VA) Primary School, Martock

My Monster Pet Jimmy

I was sat in my room, reading with
Monster Jimmy.
I turned around and I saw my sister,
I said, "Monster Jimmy, Monster Jimmy,
My sister is in my room,"
He went *roar, roar, roar*
And a *stomp, stomp, stomp.*
My sister was terrified
And she left my room,
I finished my book
And I got dressed
And I asked Monster Jimmy,
"Do you want to go to Uncle Dunkin?"
Monster Jimmy said, "I would like to,"
And we left.

Aiden Baker (9)
Martock CE (VA) Primary School, Martock

Skycloud Rabbit

S kycloud is a very special pet for me.

K at DJ is Skycloud's bestest friend ever.

Y esterday, Skycloud and Kat DJ went to the beach.

C orn and apricots and carrots are Skycloud's favourite.

L ioncorn is Kat DJ's mum, she lives in Australia.

O n the cloud is Skycloud's favourite because it is fluffy.

U nicorn is Kat DJ's second friend, they are best friends.

D ion King is very naughty, he once climbed the window.

Zeynep Akkurt (8)

Martock CE (VA) Primary School, Martock

My Peculiar Pet

I took my super dog to the shops,
But all the shoes had doggy spots,
He uses his long arms to zoom around

And sometimes blows some bubbles,
He washes my dishes and sometimes misses
And Archie and me have a cool band

And he has a friend called Eddie
He's a super dog as well
One day, Archie and me went to the beach
And when stuff is too high
He can reach it for me
And I know when he's ready
Because he puts his super-suit on!

Charlie Johnston (9)
Martock CE (VA) Primary School, Martock

Doggy Gamer, Alfie And The Hippo

At home, me and Doggy Gamer were playing
On the PlayStation.
The next day, me and Doggy Gamer
Went on holiday to France.
Stomp! Stomp! Stomp!
There was a hippo
Onboard the ferry.
Then me and Doggy Gamer got off the
Ferry and went back home.
But the hippo followed us.
Then me and Doggy Gamer looked on
The security cameras, the hippo was
Searching for us.
But it couldn't find us, so it gave
Up and exited the house.

Alfie Reynolds (9)
Martock CE (VA) Primary School, Martock

The Adventures Of Helpful Mr Owl

Helpful Mr Owl took me for a ride *very* high.
We went to France, then Big Ben, then the Statue
of Liberty.

Meanwhile, we were both *very* tired, so we took
the plane ride home
As helpful Mr Owl helped me put my stuff away.

Helpful Mr Owl fell asleep,
So cute, gentle and petite.

When we got home, he flew for the window
Now clear and see-through, although...
Too late, *splat*...
And he flew into the window.

Molly Whitelock (9)
Martock CE (VA) Primary School, Martock

Riveting Raccoon

I took my Riveting Raccoon for a walk
He is rather small and like a fool.
He is a bit sneaky and a bit cheeky.
Then I got on his back and we were off down the street
Down by the house and the trees.
He saw a big bin,
He flew me off his back and went in the bin
And I waited and waited.
We went off to the beach
He jumped on my shoulder.
Will we walk by the sea?
What a fast day!
He got his pyjamas on
And he's ready for bed.

Maxwell Taylor (9)

Martock CE (VA) Primary School, Martock

Superdog

S uperdog wears a red cape with a red mask.

U nique is the best way to describe this dog.

P layfully, he jumps for the ball

E xcitedly, he runs down the street to serve people and fight crimes.

R uffs to scare the bad guys away.

D oggies love super dogs.

O nly Superdog can save the day, he's the protector of the whole town.

G racefully, Superdog walks down the street as he's defeating the bad guys.

Gracie-May Chapman (8)

Martock CE (VA) Primary School, Martock

Fishsticks

F inding pondweed is my favourite
I love eating macaroni
S wimming is so good
H ate bananas
S o my friends think I'm weird because I only need a little pond weed
T alk a lot so I'm a chatterbox
I hate having pictures done
C alling me a fish makes me annoyed
K eeping away from evil clawy cats
S neaking under rocks in the dead of night.

Jacob Batten (8)

Martock CE (VA) Primary School, Martock

Silly Cat

My cat is silly
When we go out, most people call him Billy,
I don't know why,
It is just my mind.
I take my silly cat outside
When it's time for sunrise
When I see my cat not eating, I get surprised.
My cat can climb high.
I love it when she helps me with homework that I get set
Sometimes she helps me when I'm upset.
I love my cat
But not when she gets rats.

Olivia Cassell (9)
Martock CE (VA) Primary School, Martock

My Speedy Tortoise

I took my tortoise to the racetrack,
He's really fast.
Even if he raced against the Flash,
He would get past.
But that day, he went insane
And ran away.
He crashed into houses, he crashed into trees
And then he crashed into me!
He passed out, so did I.
We went back home with a sigh.
We went to lie down, crying out loud
And from that day onward, we never went back.

Alex Crabb (9)
Martock CE (VA) Primary School, Martock

DJ Penguin

D J likes to rock and roll.

J uggling is his favourite thing to do.

P icking his favourite song is fun.

E xcitedly, he got new juggling balls.

N ow it's DJ time!

G reat grooving music, tap to the beat, everyone!

U nder his DJ set there are loads of songs.

I n his room, he has drinks.

N ow it's time to sleep. Night!

Lexi Fane (8)

Martock CE (VA) Primary School, Martock

DJ Rofo

Rofo's friend is Dunkin and his favourite food is
pumpkin.
Rofo is a DJ, he likes to DJ in his PJs.
He sings about his PJs cos they're made of old DJ
trash
But it's not too late to crash the trash.
His other friend is called Lola and she likes
granola.
Rofo had a hat but it had a bat inside.
"Get out or I will get a net!
Are you here to get my trash?"

Elizabeth Clayton (8)
Martock CE (VA) Primary School, Martock

My Peculiar Pet

I took my robo dog to school,
He's very small and very cool,
He sneaks into my school backpack,
He's pink and blue,
His paws are black.
I take my robo dog to school,
He's very small and very cool
He's good at maths,
Which helps me out
It means my teacher doesn't shout.
I take my robo dog to school,
He's very small and very cool.

Isla Gould (9)
Martock CE (VA) Primary School, Martock

Dogalion

D ogalion likes to eat dog treats

O n the sofa, he sleeps like a lion

G oing down the street as fast as a dog

A lion so lazy he always sleeps

L ower the sofa goes thanks to Dogalion

I n the couch, this is what Dogalion's like

O n the roof, he can get down by himself

N ot going well, I need something to help Dogalion.

Jayden Ramsey (8)

Martock CE (VA) Primary School, Martock

Floppsy

F loppsy is very cheeky and cute.

L ives in a dark brown burrow.

O h, it turns into a superhero at night-time.

P ow! This bunny-headed monster can leap miles.

P ainting a purple dragon that was breathing fire.

S aw her mum and talked with her.

Y ay! Floppsy went home with her mum and ate cake.

Jack Galligan (8)
Martock CE (VA) Primary School, Martock

Cluck's Day Out!

My pet, Cluck, is good luck.
My mum likes Cluck because
Cluck tidies up.
Cluck's gentle like sand
And in my band
With a yellow guitar in his big
Soft hand.
He's big, yellow and orange and kind.
He looks grim
But he loves getting tickled on his chin.
Well, there's Cluck,
Big loveable Cluck.

Lucas Paul Pike (9)
Martock CE (VA) Primary School, Martock

Me And My Home Carry

I took my home Carry to Sloth Parthenon.
He is very strong and fast and sometimes
So slow.
He can be dangerous if you annoy him.
He can be clever and not clever.
"Come on, you need to be clever."
We are moving house, yeah
And I have my home Carry, come on.
I am so happy that I'm moving.

Mason Rendell (9)
Martock CE (VA) Primary School, Martock

Racing

R acing as fast as a rocket.
A s he zooms through the track, he flies,
C reating racing cars, eating cats in his sleep.
I n the night, he wees in his sleep.
N ow in his car, he's got a Lamborghini.
G ary, his friend, is a good friend.

Albie Fisher (8)

Martock CE (VA) Primary School, Martock

DJ

D J Dog is amazing at being a DJ.

J ogging, DJ Dog can be seen jogging around the dance floor.

D ogs, cats and lots of animals like DJ Dog's music.

O h no, DJ Dog's microphone broke and no one heard him.

G reat music, DJ Dog!

Layla Rendell (8)
Martock CE (VA) Primary School, Martock

DJ Cat

D J Cat is good at being a DJ.

J ogging around the dance floor, he has good moves.

C ats, dogs and other animals like DJ Cat's beats.

A t the disco, it was as fun as a circus.

T om is DJ Cat's real name.

Theo Taylor (8)
Martock CE (VA) Primary School, Martock

Masant

M y life is as fun as flying.

A lways hanging upside down.

S hiny ears like diamonds.

A pples make me hyper.

N o stopping my sparkling wings.

T he monkeys think that I'm one of them, but I'm not...

Diesel Hughes (8)

Martock CE (VA) Primary School, Martock

Zebkat

Z ebkat lives in a zoo

E ating apples is his favourite.

B ig, yellow and feathery Zebkat.

K eeps running around the fields.

A nteater is his best friend.

T eatime, they eat apples together.

Ashton Mcguinness (8)

Martock CE (VA) Primary School, Martock

Rocket Racoon

His name is Rocket Racoon
He likes to destroy stuff in the afternoon
He is very smelly
He has got a bomb belt on his belly.

He reloads his rocket launcher all the time
Just in case bad guys come from the sky.

Connor Dervishi (8)

Martock CE (VA) Primary School, Martock

My Peculiar Pet

Gerry is very tall
And very large
With brown spots.
He rescues me
When I'm stuck in a tree.
He makes a good goalkeeper,
Still playing football
Gerry, Gerry, the ball-getter.

Mason Woodhouse (9)

Martock CE (VA) Primary School, Martock

Crocodragon

Crocodragon is thirty metres
Longer than a normal crocodile.

Crocodragon was supposed to be extinct
100,000,000 years ago.

Oliver Harding (8)
Martock CE (VA) Primary School, Martock

Lion

L ong hairy mane.
I nto the woods he hides
O ver the logs he pounces
N o other animal is there.

Ronnie Bouckley (8)
Martock CE (VA) Primary School, Martock

Meersnake

My peculiar pet is a meersnake
His favourite thing is cake
He loves being underground
Because it has no sound.

Freddie Frost (8)
Martock CE (VA) Primary School, Martock

About The Favourite Cat

I have a cat
She is the fluffiest cat
She is the nicest cat
She is the best cat
I play with her
Sometimes I play with her in the garden
Sometimes I put a lead on her
And walk around the park
She is the bestest cat in the world
I love her so much
She all the time plays catch with me.
She is my favourite cat in the world
My cat says, "Miaow!" so loud
And tastes things if she wants to.

Ayesha Kanwar (7)
Millbrook Combined School, High Wycombe

Little Rabbits And Bunnies

I can see some cute rabbits and bunnies
And a sunset
The sunsets are beautiful
And I felt so happy that I got a flute and played
the flute
The bunnies and the rabbits were happy
They made a queue
I can hear the cute noises of the rabbits and
bunnies
And the crying bunnies
They make me sad.
I can smell the beautiful smell of the
Rabbits and bunnies.

Amaya Qureshi (6)
Millbrook Combined School, High Wycombe

About Bunny

I hear my bunny hopping around the garden
She is lovely, I love her.
She is hopping very high.
She has a heart-shaped nose
It is so cute
She has shoes but she does not wear them
And her coat.
She goes everywhere with me
She has a normal dress and a party dress
Her party dress is pink
Her normal dress has squares that are rainbow.

Julia Gulacsi (6)
Millbrook Combined School, High Wycombe

Secret Sparkly Land

Once, in Secret Sparkly Land,
There was a bunny called Bany.
She loves to play games
Like basketball, football, volleyball and cricket.
She always likes to draw pictures
Of her castle and me.
Bany sometimes is unhappy with me.

Gabriela Grudzinska (7)
Millbrook Combined School, High Wycombe

Peculiar Pets

I can hear the owl hoot hoot at midnight.
The owls fly to find food.
They like to sleep all day and hunt all night.
I can see their big orange eyes.
Their heads move round and round.
Owls have a good sense of smell.

Ruqaiyyah-Fatimah Kousar (7)
Millbrook Combined School, High Wycombe

Lions

I hear lions,
They sound loud!
I see lions,
They look furry and they look scary,
And a little cute.
I smell lions,
They smell stinky.
Lions taste a little tasty.

George Digby (7)
Millbrook Combined School, High Wycombe

The Vegetarian Tiger, Vegie-Spikes

V ulnerable, fear raced through the monotonous mind of Vegie-Spikes as quick as a lightning-fast cheetah.

E very day, the old tiger got the cursed thoughts of being non-vegetarian, which he feared

G reatly scared of meat, he added another weird feature to himself all those years ago

I ncredibly, his ferocious family had taken his peculiar perspective towards meat rather well

E ntering the world of vegetarians, he was cursed with the sickening spell of doubt - he stuck with his choice

S oon, the spell had taken over Vegie-Spikes' white and blue body

P eacocks saw through him, kangaroos jumped onto him and lions hunted him

I n fear, one day, he asked the lions why he was getting hunted and the leader lioness replied with the words: "If you are not one of us, then you will be the prey."

K angaroos jumped onto him, not because they couldn't see him, but because they mocked him for not belonging in any animal family

E xpectedly, Vegie-Spikes died and got eaten by lanky lions

S eries of unfortunate events happened to Vegie-Spikes, but right now he is resting in peace.

Nyma Jawwad (10)
New Hall Primary & Children's Centre, Sutton Coldfield

The Peculiar Perry

P erfect gymnast.

E xcellent at making you smile, ridiculous routines to make you laugh.

C reative and caring at all times.

U nique and proud of it.

L ovely when making you happy.

I n a garden is where you will find him.

A magical little creature waiting for its berries

R ather fun they are and kind

P eculiar look but stands out in the crowd

E very time you smile, he grows a smile too!

R eally here to make friends

R eversing his past ends

Y ou know he loves you, so say hello!

Ashia Hanley (10)
New Hall Primary & Children's Centre, Sutton Coldfield

My Guinea Pig's Delight

Fast asleep in my lavish bed
In comes a girl's head!
She traps the exit with her hand
Scoops up my sassy sister and
Clever me! I run for it!

I go up and down
Round and round
Into my tunnel
Then in comes a hand!

The hand is like a claw machine
Scooping me up like a prize.

Clutched to her chest
We stare eye to eye
In her other hand
Lovely carrots nearby!

As I leap like a tiger onto the soggy grass
The juicy carrots are mine at last!

Elsie Taylor (9)
New Hall Primary & Children's Centre, Sutton Coldfield

The Bird That Is Scared To Fly!

Have you ever wondered
'Bout a bird scared to fly,
That dreads to even take a step
Out into the sky?
Well, listen to me, everyone,
I know a bird like that,
It's a blue-crested, red-chested bird with a very tall hat.
It has all the normal qualities a bird already has,
Apart from the one that makes other birds real mad.
You might be thinking
Oh, it's not so bad,
But for the great big bird gang,
It's pretty sad.

Joshika-Gauri Surgu (10)
New Hall Primary & Children's Centre, Sutton Coldfield

Penelope Panda

P enelope Panda is my flying furry friend.

E ven though she is an animal,

N o one can replace my cheeky clawed companion.

E very day we hang out just like inseparable, imaginative sisters and we

L ive together on the island of Crete.

O nly my adorable, adventurous ally can dig deeper than any known species.

P rancing round for precious prey is her main hobby, but I love

E ntertaining little children.

Neva Giby (10)

New Hall Primary & Children's Centre, Sutton Coldfield

The Poem Of The Different-Looking Chicken

Hiding from his enemies, he didn't want revenge.
Yesterday, he couldn't sleep, his enemies didn't feel any guilt.
Bins, closets, rooms, basements and the roof; he couldn't hide,
Ruining his life, he now was filled with rage.
It didn't help him be kind, it made him mad.
Did anything help? It couldn't; he went berserk.
His bullies regret the thing they did
His trap worked, *kapow!*
He went without a doubt.

Maksymillian (10)

New Hall Primary & Children's Centre, Sutton Coldfield

The See-Through Elephant

There once was a see-through elephant called
Morgan.
You could always see her organs.
She was very very kind.
But one time I lost her and she was very hard to
find.
Morgan was my very best friend,
And I found her in the West End.
I would never replace her or my face would go red.
You could see her bones,
And every time she was bored, she groaned.
I very well saw her lungs and she breathed in lots,
tons.

Karma Salama (10)
New Hall Primary & Children's Centre, Sutton Coldfield

Coco Fish

F ields filled with snow

R andom fish in hot cocoa

O pportunity for a cold buddy like me

S eeing the world would be a dream come true

T hings he does

Y ou will shriek

C oughing from the cold

H ot cocoa warms up his world

O nward for a new chapter

C oco will be here forever.

Kawther Mahdi (10)

New Hall Primary & Children's Centre, Sutton Coldfield

My Best Friend

Hi, my name is Chloe, this is my narwhal, she can fly.
She is my best friend, she is owned by me and she is mine.
Narwhals are cute, she was the size of a shampoo bottle.
She is so cute that I named her Cotton.
Now she is so big, like the size of a whale.
She is now the biggest female.
She is so adorable.
She is very sassy.
She loves all the fascinating colours, she is very messy.
She is the cutest animal of all.
We love to shop at the mall.
She flies all day.
She loves me.

Aaliyah Fasanya (8)
Nightingale Primary School, Hackney

My Blue Sloth

I have a sloth called Ruby
She likes to dance to the boogie
Her favourite fruit is mango
She loves to Tango

Ruby is sweet and cuddly
She is my best buddy
At night, we sleep together
And I hope it's forever

Every time I see her, I feel joy in my heart
We love to draw and do art
When she eats her food, she eats very slow
Broccoli, salad and peas make her grow
She likes to tell jokes and be funny, and her
nickname is Honey!

Gabriella Parker (8)
Nightingale Primary School, Hackney

Wild Wolf And Me

I have a pet called Wild Wolf
She is fluffy and cute but fierce
She wears a face mask
And spy's clothes.
She's got very sharp claws
And teeth that could regrow.
Three layers of skin on her chin.
Wanna know how to tame her? I guess
Just take it easy, no stress
You might not adore her, but I
Do.
Wild Wolf, my siblings and me.

Khadijah Njie (8)
Nightingale Primary School, Hackney

My Cheeky Panda

I have a panda
Her name is Amanda

She is very cheeky
And is kind of dreamy

She likes to cuddle
And jump in puddles

As she dreams, she sees the sky
And jumps really high

All I know
Is that she loves me so.

Maariyah Mirza (8)
Nightingale Primary School, Hackney

Frosty

My pet is called Frosty
He is so cosy
He loves the cold
And doesn't like mould
Frosty is big
And I put it on a rug
I threw a ball
And it hit the wall
Frosty thought I was his dad
When I said I wasn't, he got all mad...

Ryuto Hashimoto Huynh (8)
Nightingale Primary School, Hackney

Hortle's Trip To The Past

Happy all the time
And loves to climb
No more time to whine
Grab your boots
And your suits
Ready, steady, go, go, go!

We're off on a blast
To go to the past.
Look, it's me over there
I'm playing and neighing everywhere.

Poor old Hortle, you have to go home
Back to the future
To be with Zeutur.
Zoom, boom, beep, beep!

Yes, we're back to the present
And everything's pleasant.
Feeling tired, he sends himself
Snoozing and snoring.

Tiffany-Lou Paget (10)
Perry Court E-ACT Academy, Hengrove

Janitor Cat

J anitor Cat is a big, fat, round, hairy and cuddly ginger cat who cleans my school.

A fter school, he cleans and sweeps the classroom floors with his big, bushy, ginger tail.

N ext, he cleans any small spaces with his long sharp claws.

I f he forgets his glasses, he can't see, so the school won't be clean for the morning

T hough he always tries his best to keep everywhere clean using the hair

O n his big, bushy, ginger tail, he always leaves a trail of ginger fur behind him.

R ing! went the end-of-school bell, time to

C lean the windows. Silly children had got the windows

A ll muddy, so Janitor Cat licked them nice and clean with his pink and blue

T ongue.

Tabitha Wright (9)

St Benedict's Catholic Primary School, Hindley

The Crazy, Cat-Burgling Corgi!

Queen Elizabeth II, was about to be in so much trouble.
She had left Buckingham Palace, to visit her COVID bubble.
She had left her chief corgi asleep on her throne,
When he awoke, he found that nobody was home.
She didn't take him with her which made him feel all down,
He knew there was only one thing he now wanted: that was her crown!

So, off he went on a journey to the Tower of London,
Where all of his fun would start all of a sudden.
He passed the Beefeater, stood to attention at the gate
And stole a quick snack from the raven's food plate.
He made his way oh so quietly up to the crown jewel room,
But on his way, he was frightened by the sound of an enormous vacuum.

He turned and ran as quick as he could,
Scared that his Queen may have misunderstood.
He ran to the Palace, over the fence and past the Queen's guard,
Hoping the Queen would not find out and say he was barred.
He was so worried and upset at what he had done,
As the Queen was so nice, kind and so much fun.

Isaac Wright (11)
St Benedict's Catholic Primary School, Hindley

Tom, Arthur And Licorice

Tom, Arthur and Licorice are my cats
Tom and Arthur are as ginger as the sun
Licorice is as black as the night
Tom and Arthur catch mice
Licorice is too slow and old
Arthur sleeps like a frog with his legs stretched out
Tom brings us presents of butterflies and mice
Tom, Arthur and Licorice like to eat smelly food
They smell of fish
Tom, Arthur and Licorice are my cats
I love them.

Natalia Campbell (7)

St Gregory's Catholic Primary School, Margate

Fluffy, My Lovely Bunny

Fluffy smells like a flower,
A bit like a rose.
Fluffy looks black and
A bit of peach on the neck.
Fluffy feels cosy
And soft like a pillow.
Fluffy's eyes are black
And brown.
When Fluffy breathes, he sounds
Like he is
Breathing really fast.

I love Fluffy.

Annie Rajive (7)

St Gregory's Catholic Primary School, Margate

My Dog Molly

Molly looks like twenty cute teddies
And as white as a cloud.

Molly smells like thirty-five fishes.
Molly sounds like two dogs barking for twelve
hours...

Molly feels like a big soft cloud.
Molly tastes like a catfish wrapped in hair.

Dami Olulode (7)
St Gregory's Catholic Primary School, Margate

Polly My Dog

Polly smells like rotten food and fish organs.
Polly looks as white as snow and as grey as tools.
Polly sounds a bit loud when people come in.
Polly feels like material that's soft.
Polly tastes like burnt meat.
Polly is my best dog buddy.

Poppy Queen (7)
St Gregory's Catholic Primary School, Margate

My Peculiar Pet

My chicken is soft, just like my bed
And it's cuddly like a cuddly toy.
My chicken smells fishy and dirty.
It tastes juicy and it tastes like lemon.
It looks furry and cute and looks lovely.
It sounds annoying but beautiful and kind.

Tatum Gower (6)
St Gregory's Catholic Primary School, Margate

Raja, My Favourite Dog

Raja tastes like ice cream
Raja smells like ice cream
Raja feels like a teddy bear and some fur
Raja looks as black as midnight
Raja sounds like a creaky door

I love you so much, Raja.

Swanika Kanesarasa (6)
St Gregory's Catholic Primary School, Margate

My Alicorn

Rosilina is an alicorn.

Rosilina smells sweet.

Rosilina feels soft and warm.

Rosilina sounds smooth and calm and happy.

Rosilina tastes like rainbow cupcakes.

Rosilina looks happy and sweet.

Astrid Binu (7)

St Gregory's Catholic Primary School, Margate

My Owl

My owl smells like daisies.
My owl looks like a light grey.
My owl sounds like what any other bird sounds
like.
My owl feels *sooo* soft.
My owl tastes like roast chicken.

Emma Abraham (6)

St Gregory's Catholic Primary School, Margate

Fluffy

Fluffy smells like blossom and roses.
Fluffy looks grey and white.
Fluffy sounds like water dripping from the taps.
Fluffy eats rabbit mix.
Fluffy drinks milk.

Alana Hobley (7)
St Gregory's Catholic Primary School, Margate

My Flying Pet Cookie

F lying Cookie is my pet.

L oving Cookie loves cupcakes with extra icing and a cherry on top.

Y ellow feathers drift around her which she loves to get.

I cing is Cookie's favourite thing on a cupcake.

N othing stops Cookie from having fun in the shop.

G oing to get ice cream is her favourite and she always gets a Flake.

C ooking treats is what she does on Fridays when I'm away.

O nce every week, I would play with her all day.

O nce every month, she would let me ride on her back to see the sunset.

K aren sometimes tried to get us wet.

I n the middle of the day, there would be some cake and fruit for her, of course.

E very Thursday, I would take her to my horse riding lessons with my horse.

Demi-Rose Marlow (8)
Wildground Junior School, Dibden Purlieu

Super Stripes

S urprisingly, a new supercat had arrived!

U p! Up! Up! He flew high in the sky.

P lants grew higher and higher, this supercat is a hero!

E verybody cheered and took selfies with him.

"R eady to fly!" he cried and launched off.

S uper Stripes is his name, cheer for Super Stripes!

T remendous cheering flew in the air.

R ecklessly, he grabbed an ink bottle to fill up a pen

I n an apartment, someone screamed!

P encils fell out the window.

"E eeahchch!" The person had her leg stuck in a chair!

S uper Stripes used his super strength to get the foot out.

"Thank you," said the person.

"You're most welcome!" cried Super Stripes.

Eddie Anderson (8)

Wildground Junior School, Dibden Purlieu

My Mad Pet

My mad pet is the most mad of them all,
Whenever I say, "Boo," he wildly falls!

If I sit on the sofa in his favourite spot,
He will growl and pounce and make me very hot.

We go for a walk (always on his skateboard)
Then he goes too far and passes the house of the Lord.

I have to keep buying new sunglasses every day,
But each time I do, Ralph takes them away.

Why does my dog's snout look like a pig's nose?
I guess it was just the way he was made, but what if it wasn't?
Nobody knows.

He hates the zoo because of the animals,
Especially the elephants, they look like big cannibals!

This is why my pet is the most mad of them all,
By the way, he is very tall.

Isla Burrow (8)
Wildground Junior School, Dibden Purlieu

Super Charly!

S omeone come here, guess what? My cat's a superhero.

U p she goes, saves animals and the world, listen, you!

P ants in the town of wonder, Charly go save poo!

E mily the dirty poodle leaves trash everywhere so dirty

R obert calls Charly to get Poodle, she's called Captain Dirty!

C harly and Birty always work together to save the Earth

H ey, everyone! Guess what? My cat's friend is Birty

A nd now we should know my cat's a princess diamond

R ock 'n' roll Charly, come and play on an island

L ook, my cat is riding on yummy-so-yum honey!

Y ou, look! Have you heard the big news? My cat is making money!

Charlotte Newcombe (8)

Wildground Junior School, Dibden Purlieu

Super Stanley

S uper Stanley is amazing at dancing,

U nder the dirt in Stanley's house was Stanley sleeping there.

P erfect house for Stanley.

E ven though Stanley is a tortoise, he can dance.

R ight, you don't believe me?

S uper Stanley is the best to me

T he thing I love about Stanley is that he's kind, call him Kind Stanley if you want.

A n amazing thing once happened to me.

N o, no, no, I keep getting this poem all wrong.

L et me try again next time.

E ven though I practise lots, I still get it wrong

Y ct I've written 1,002 of these!

Alba Bunday (8)

Wildground Junior School, Dibden Purlieu

Kayla The Singer

K ayla loves to sing for her fans

A piano is her fave instrument to play all day

Y ou can sing with her, you can dance with her

L ove is what she shares

A ll she cares about is pears

T ea is her number-one drink

H er dress has roses on

E lephants in the show, everyone was amazed

S assy is her name

I n the performance, she freaked out, she saw Katy P

"N o way!" she cried

G reen was everywhere

E veryone left in amazement

R emember she's the best singer.

Elise Valman
Wildground Junior School, Dibden Purlieu

My Slimy Friend

There was one dragon named Ice Titan
He was having a good time at school
Suddenly a flash struck as fast as a racing
motorcycle
Then something wild happened
A slimy person was walking sassily around
Then something happened to the dragon Ice Titan
And he turned into a warrior
Then he was wild and clever
Then he went up to the slimy person
He was very brave
He approached and it was a
Dragon dripping slime
Ice Titan become friends with him
He was playing with him and his other friends.

Lucas Zaharia (7)
Wildground Junior School, Dibden Purlieu

My Peculiar Pet

Hissing Hilda came to school
Apparently, she was very cool
She climbed a tree
And got an apple for me
She can become a fairy
Her fur is not too hairy
Excitable every day
Just ask her to come and play
Stars on her headband
She loves sitting in the sand
She chases moles
She chases voles
Has her love for foals
She never gives up her goals

Is she a cat?

Hazel Baxter (8)
Wildground Junior School, Dibden Purlieu

Super Cat

S uper Cat is on a roll and a stroll.

U p he goes, there he flows.

P ut the Cat Car in invisible mode!

E nter the bank, they go in rank.

"R ight, where's the car?" said the villain.

C at Car is cool, it's hidden from the fool!

A mazing Super Cat is a blazing Super Cat.

T op form from the Cat Car.

Ryan C Windebank (8)

Wildground Junior School, Dibden Purlieu

About My Dog

D ummy
U nattractive
G rizzly when we come home
G rumpy when he's on the couch
E xcited at dinnertime
E very day goes crazy.

T errible with his nose
H ears a lot
E ats anything

D umps anywhere
U nbelievably stupid
M ale
B umps into stuff, ouch!

Ethan Parker
Wildground Junior School, Dibden Purlieu

Matilda The Snow Dog

Matilda and I were just waking up
Out of my cosy purple bed.
I was bored, I asked her to make some snow
And off we did go.
We were playing in the cold snow.
It was cold like the North Pole.
Then, after, we had some fun
And bye-bye cold fun day.
It was the most fun day
Like my birthday.
It was hard to get home
Like digging a big hole.

Eleyna Carvalho (8)
Wildground Junior School, Dibden Purlieu

DJ Dinosaur

D on't touch DJ Bold Man

J ust make some wicked songs.

B eware of the DJ

O ne, two, now it's DJ time

L and in DJ room, yo

D J Bold Man playing a fighting DJ match

M y friend and me are going to a party

A pretty party with DJ Bold Man

N o jazz music; wicked music.

Osea Kamakorewa (7)

Wildground Junior School, Dibden Purlieu

DJ Poppy

D one all the songs on the list

J umping up and down to the beat but the next one they all missed.

P ong! it went, something is wrong

O ver and over again it went bong!

P ing! Poppy had an idea

P oppy first gave everyone a beer

Y ay! Poppy fixed it, hooray for her, on her way home she licked her fur.

Joe Hoyle
Wildground Junior School, Dibden Purlieu

Flying Giraffe

F lying in the sky.
L ow to the ground.
Y ou have to come and see!
I t's always moving around.
N owhere it's really going.
G oing as slow as a snail.

F red is its name.
R iding in the air.
E nding where it wants to go.
D one with flying and goes to bed.

Theodore Knowlton (8)

Wildground Junior School, Dibden Purlieu

Peculiar Pet Pishu

P ishu the panda found some Fanta.

I t has some bubbly texture.

S o, he got sick because he drank the Fanta and he's allergic to Fanta!

H e is all right now and he's going to the shop to buy a different drink.

U gly drinks are bad, so never drink them, my panda friends.

Leo Mark Hamilton (8)
Wildground Junior School, Dibden Purlieu

Stripy Tail

S tripy likes being stroked
T o be happy
R unning in the garden
I n and out the trees
P urring and playing with a mouse
Y oung, cute kitten

T all is Stripy
A dventurous kitten
I s messy and clever
L ove my kitten!

Roan Wells (8)
Wildground Junior School, Dibden Purlieu

My Peculiar Pet

D angerously, Domino was riding his skateboard

O lly's first friend was Domino.

M y cat is the best at skateboarding.

I ce cream is the best for my cat.

N emo is Domino's best friend.

O n the weekend, he plays with me.

Molly Paddock (8)

Wildground Junior School, Dibden Purlieu

Dog Man's Odd Day

D og Man is great in every way

O n a journey through nature

G ood Dog Man goes on an adventure.

M orning is here

A nd there's a terrible disaster

N ow Dog Man has the power to have giant ears that make him fly.

Isaac Campbell (8)

Wildground Junior School, Dibden Purlieu

Simba's Show

S imba was a lion lying in his cabin

I t's time for a show to find his glow

M aybe he'll be rich after

B ang! Dum-bum, dum-bum

A fter the show, Simba got trampled by fans and everyone loved him.

Maiya Ferguson (8)
Wildground Junior School, Dibden Purlieu

Muddy Buddy

B uddy was a dog lying in a bog,

U gly Buddy is very muddy.

D ogs are clever, they love the weather

D o your dogs do this stuff? Because they can be rough.

Y our dogs are young, they can still be fun.

Hetty Bliss (8)

Wildground Junior School, Dibden Purlieu

The Lazy Cat

A lazy cat who is crazy.
She walked to school and
Cooked a pancake.
She put it on her head
It was sticky and
Messy.
It was night.
She had a shower.
She went to bed for a rest
She yawned
Sleep time!

Bella-Rose Knightbridge (8)

Wildground Junior School, Dibden Purlieu

Frog Saves The Day

M r Frog can fly by using his cape,
R ide Mr Frog to be safe.

F rogs are flying over the Earth.
R ide him to save the day.
O h my god... bang!
G row bigger, you're too small.

Harley Baylis (7)

Wildground Junior School, Dibden Purlieu

My Missy

M y Missy is yellow with a fluffy long tail
I love it when I get a ride on her soft fur.
S he sounds sweet with her lovely miaow
S eeing her soar is a wonderful sight
Y es, she is the best.

Evelyn Havers (8)
Wildground Junior School, Dibden Purlieu

My One And Only Frank!

F rank, my best friend forever.

R eal ninja, always there for people.

A wesome pet, crash! He's there.

N injatastic, as brave as a lion slaying bad guys.

K ind, my one and only Frank.

Jethro Kendie (8)

Wildground Junior School, Dibden Purlieu

DJ Rocky

D angerous DJ Rocky
J ammed the disc on the

R usty deck. He switched it
O n and then it
C racked!
K icking the deck, DJ Rocky
Y elled and went wild.

Heidi Woodhead

Wildground Junior School, Dibden Purlieu

Ranker Cow

R unner - this cow can run.

A dorable and cute.

N apper - she likes to nap.

K ind and clumsy

E xcellent and clever

R ecorder - she can play this to her friends.

Noah Tollervey (8)

Wildground Junior School, Dibden Purlieu

D J Meow

D ancing across the DJ floor.

J oy is happy to have.

M eat is a treat

E gg is the best to have.

O n the DJ floor, he fell over.

W e played together.

Leo Elsley

Wildground Junior School, Dibden Purlieu

Sumbo The Clown Dog

Today, I went to the circus,
Suddenly, a dastardly dog came out.
He was crazy!
I spoke to the host, then ran home.
I had a drink and then had dinner.
After that, I went to sleep.

James McIldoon (7)

Wildground Junior School, Dibden Purlieu

The Crazy Racoon

R ocky the Racoon is small

O n his teeny little legs

C an he fly? Yes, he can

K nows a lot of tricks, a lot of them

Y olk of an egg is his fave food.

Emily Gahr (7)

Wildground Junior School, Dibden Purlieu

DJ Croc

D ancing he loves
J uicy meat is a treat for him

C ool
R ecording himself, he is really good
O ctopus is his best friend
C lever.

Joseph Mitchell (7)
Wildground Junior School, Dibden Purlieu

Dizzy Lizzy

Today, I went to the pet shop.
There was only one pet left.
A snake, a python - Dizzy Lizzy.
She made me dizzy.
Oh, Dizzy Lizzy.

Tiana-Rae Smith (8)
Wildground Junior School, Dibden Purlieu

Panda Man The Hero

Panda Man saved the city
For the robbers, it's a pity
Panda Man is so smart
He was the part
Now he is known as Super Panda!

Andrew-John Smith (8)
Wildground Junior School, Dibden Purlieu

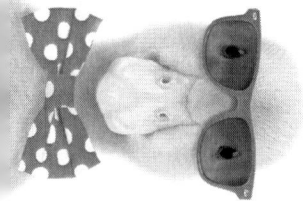

George The Flying Monkey

He walks, he glides, he swoops, he climbs
The one and only George flies by.
His tail is curly, his wings are strong.
He'll pick your pocket as you go along.
He walks, he glides, he swoops, he climbs
My pet, the flying monkey, flies by.

Luke Ryan Spendlove (11)
Woodlands School, Great Warley